Living In
OVERFLOW

FROM LACK TO ABUNDANCE JOURNAL

DR. LEAH MCCRAY

"BELOVED, I WISH (PRAY) ABOVE ALL THINGS THAT YOU MAY PROSPER AND BE IN HEALTH, EVEN AS YOUR SOUL PROSPERS." 3 JOHN 2

What does it mean to prosper? What does it mean to live in overflow?

Most simply, it means to have more than enough; to have sufficiency of supply, to lack nothing.
But, what we also learn from this scripture is that it starts from within and flows outward.

For the next 21 days we will submerse ourselves in the word of God concerning provision and we will root out the spirits of poverty, pride and penny pinching to emerge a truly prosperous soul, inside and out.

God wants you to prosper
Jeremiah 29:11

DAY 1

Read this verse and let it sink into your heart. In what areas of your life have you settled for less than God's best? In your own words, write what prosperity in those areas would look like to you.

_____
_____
_____
_____
_____
_____
_____
_____

Action steps to walk out this revelation:

1.
2.
3.

He's Greater

DAY 2

Psalm 47: 1-9

How are you viewing your God, the only God of heaven and earth? There is no one or no thing greater! Write down the challenges that you are currently experiencing.. List every battle, each and every stronghold where you have yet to see victory.

_____
_____
_____
_____
_____
_____
_____
_____
_____
_____

Action steps to walk out this revelation:

1.
2.
3.

Clean hands

DAY 3

1 John 1:9

Before you can prosper on the inside or out, you must confess any unforgiveness, jealousy, malice and any other sin that you have been hiding in your heart. Nothing will work until you free yourself from Satan's clutches. We do this by coming clean and asking God for forgiveness. Take some time to search your heart and write a letter to your Daddy confessing all. You won't believe the blessing that will come because of it.

Action steps to walk out this revelation:

1.

2.

3.

First things

Matthew 6:33

DAY 4

Prosperity is not born in chaos. There is a divine order to everything and there are principles that we must uphold to usher in the favor and abundance of God. Chief among them is to put God first. Write down the ways that you can begin to seek God first before anything else.

_____

_____

_____

_____

_____

_____

_____

_____

_____

_____

Action steps to walk out this revelation:

1.

2.

3.

The faith factor

Mark 11:22-24

DAY 5

You must believe. There is no getting around this. Faith is required! How can we acknowledge so great a God and not believe what He says? Activate your faith in all areas of your life and watch what happens. Where have you doubted God in your area of finances? What are you willing to do today to increase your faith so that you can live today's verse?

Action steps to walk out this revelation:

1.
2.
3.

One source Many channels

DAY 6

Genesis 22:13-14

God alone is the source of whatever you need and He may use many different channels to get you the supply. Understanding that every good and perfect gift comes from God is the first step in helping you to not look to your own ability, or the ability of others, but to look to Him who is able to make what is required appear exactly when needed. In what ways have you not acted in the understanding of this truth, and what will you do with this revelation?

_____

_____

_____

_____

_____

_____

_____

Action steps to walk out this revelation:

1.

2.

3.

The power of a dime

Malachi 3:10

Don't let ten cents stand in the way of your abundance. Why would you give ten pennies the power to cause you to live in lack? When you disobey God in the tithe, that is what you are doing. God doesn't need your money, but He does require your faith to obey. Write down your thoughts about tithing and ask God to increase your faith and revelation.

DAY 7

Action steps to walk out this revelation:

1.

2.

3.

The seeds you scatter

DAY 8

Luke 6:38

The principle of this world is to take and withhold; that's how you grow your accounts and ward off lack. However, in God's economy, which is the only one that matters, you increase and grow wealth by giving. Yes, it's antithetical to this world view, but it is truth. In what ways have you withheld out of fear and in what ways will you change to align yourself with this revelation?

_____

_____

_____

_____

_____

_____

_____

_____

Action steps to walk out this revelation:

1.
2.
3.

Willing & obedient

Isiah 1:19

Being prosperous and remaining in a state of prosperity comes with certain conditions. As you read and meditate on today's verse, ask God to show you any areas where you may have been obedient, but you have not been willing. Both must be present for full abundance. Repent and ask God to give you action steps to help you let go of reluctance.

DAY 9

Action steps to walk out this revelation:

1.
2.
3.

What do you want

Matthew 7:7

DAY 10

Before you petition the throne room of God, you must have specific requests. Don't go to Him with vague supplications, know exactly what you are desiring from your Father, and ask him to release it to you. And, once you ask, keep on asking, not as one in fear of not receiving, but as one excited about the day you will see your request manifested in your life. What are you asking for today concerning your finances and what action steps will you take to be in aligned to this word?

_____

_____

_____

_____

_____

_____

_____

_____

Action steps to walk out this revelation:

1.

2.

3.

Release your imagination

Ephesians 3:20

DAY 11

Take a few moments to let your mind run free. Remove any barriers and all boundaries. See your life exactly how you would like it to be. See poverty and lack removed completely. What does your life look like? Write your vision down, but, understand that God can do so much more in you and for you than what you have imagined, if you let Him. He wants you to prosper!

_____
_____
_____
_____
_____
_____
_____
_____

Action steps to walk out this revelation:

1.
2.
3.

Unlimited supply

Phillipians 4:19

DAY 12

In the natural world, supply is limited and resources can be depleted. However, in God's economy, there is unlimited supply. This means that what you are able to receive is never limited by the quantity of what another has acquired. There are endless pieces in this pie. This revelation should free you from any spirit of covetousness and give you peace, knowing that God is able to supply ALL of your needs. Write about some ways you believe this revelation will transform the way you think about money and having your needs met.

_____

_____

_____

_____

_____

_____

_____

_____

Action steps to walk out this revelation:

1.
2.
3.

Law of multiplication

DAY 13

Mark 10:28-31

It may often feel like to follow God's word is to always be giving something up; surrendering something that you value. And, in a large part this is true. Especially when we put more value on the things of this world than on spiritual thngs. However, this verse is a promise from our Lord that whatever you give up in pursuit of following and obeying Him, you will get it back MULTIPLIED, in this world. So. don't believe the lie that God wants to take from you. What He is really trying to do is INCREASE you. Take some time to write whatever is coming up in your heart as you think about this revelation, then list some action steps that you will take to walk this truth out in your life.

___

___

___

___

___

___

Action steps to walk out this revelation:

1.
2.
3.

Debt cancellation

DAY 14

Matthew 18:27

Throughout the Bible, you will find examples showing the heart of our Father to cancel the debt of his children. In fact, He instituted a law to cancel all debt every seventh and fiftieth year. So, if today, you find yourself steeped in debt, for whatever reason, just know that God wants you to be free of it. AND more importantly, He wants you to understand that when in debt you are a slave to it.

_____

_____

_____

_____

_____

_____

_____

_____

Action steps to walk out this revelation:

1.
2.
3.

Expect your harvest

DAY 15

Gen. 8:22, Mark 4:26-32

It is a natural and spiritual law, that whatever you plant, you shall also reap. God also lets us know that there is no time limit on our sowing, so keep waiting, keep looking, keep EXPECTING! It shall come and it shall not tarry. What have you been praying and sowing for? Write it down along with your prayer and declaration of agreement that His word never returns void.

_____

_____

_____

_____

_____

_____

_____

_____

Action steps to walk out this revelation:

1.
2.
3.

Don't waiver

DAY 16

James 1:5-7

God says that he will give us the ability, the know how, the wisdom to create wealth (Deut. 8:18). But He also tells us that we cannot operate and flow in His wisdom in the midst of doubt. What challenges are you facing in truly trusting and believing His word? It's okay to admit them. He knew that the forces of hell would come against our faith. Write whatever Holy Spirit brings to mind and then ask God for the wisdom to overcome those areas and walk in victory.

Action steps to walk out this revelation:

1.
2.
3.

You first

Genesis 13:8-12

DAY 17

Another key to overflow is practicing the art of deference. In our scripture reference, we see Abraham living this out. Instead of trying to keep the best for himself, he chose the route of peace and allowed Lot to choose. He could do this in confidence because he knew that his blessings came from God. Can you recall some areas of your life or some decisions you have made where you did not practice this? Take some time to ask God for forgiveness. In what ways can you begin to live this practice out in your life? Walking in this revelation is a key to unlocking your prosperous season.

Action steps to walk out this revelation:

1.
2.
3.

Repair the breach

DAY 18

Psalm 37:25 Your inheritance is that you will never have to beg for what you need. Lack is not your portion. So, if we are not seeing this promise manifested in our lives, let's check our hearts first. If there is unconfessed sin, let's deal with it. After that, let's check our hands. What are we doing in the natural? Are we making wise financial decisions? Are we spending beyond where we are right now? Pray and ask Holy Spirit to reveal any areas in need of repair and write down what you hear. God wants you to live in abundance, let Him show you how.

Action steps to walk out this revelation:

1.
2.
3.

Stare it down

DAY 19

Matthew 13:21

Afflictions come because of the word of truth. You have come a long way in transforming your mind to the word of God regarding prosperity and the enemy wants you to quit, to back down, to give up. Don't be surprised by any unexpected expense or set-back. Just keep doing what you know to do and God will turn it all around for your good. Write down anything that is trying to hinder you and take your peace. Declare that God is working it all out for your good and His glory.

Action steps to walk out this revelation:

1.
2.
3.

It's a game changer

Psalm 37:25

DAY 20

You have a distinct advantage in life and that supernatural edge is called **FAVOR**! It is that "secret sauce" that causes those in the world to scratch their heads and wonder how can you come out of a mess with a message? Emerge from a test with a testimony? Why does it always seem to work out for you? It's the favor of God! It's more precious than gold and it's always working on your behalf. In what areas do you clearly see God's favor at work in your life? In what areas do you want to see God's favor intervene? Journal it and watch God begin to reveal more of how His favor is at work in your life.

_____

_____

_____

_____

_____

_____

Action steps to walk out this revelation:

1.
2.
3.

Jehovah Jireh

Genesis 22:13-18

DAY 21

There is so much in this Name! We generally translate this as "the Lord will provide," and this is essentially correct, but the Hebraic words used for this wonderful attribute of God goes so much further. It literally means that He is the one who looks ahead to where He has you walking in life and makes sure that when you get to that place of need, the supply is waiting for you. This is PROVISION. He provides for the vision BEFORE the vision. What an awesome God! Write down the many ways that you have seen God meet your needs over the past 21 days and thank Him for all He has done and all He will do! You are blessed and you are PROSPEROUS1

_____

_____

_____

_____

_____

_____

_____

Action steps to walk out this revelation:

1.
2.
3.

PUTTING IT ALL TOGETHER

What I've learned about God:

What I've learned about me:

What has happened during these 21 days:

I want to challenge myself in these areas to reach my next level of faith:

Declarations

Thank YOU!

I pray that this journal has been a blessing to you and I encourage you to always remember that
YOU ARE PROSPEROUS.
Why?
Because, your Daddy owns everything in heaven and in the earth,
AND,
it is His good pleasure to take good care of you!

Min. Leah

www.ingramcontent.com/pod-product-compliance
Lightning Source LLC
Chambersburg PA
CBHW081330040426
42453CB00013B/2368